WHEN THE CLOCK STRIKES TWELVE

By: Antwoun Stevens

☐

When The Clock Strikes Twelve

When The Clock Strikes Twelve

☐

When The Clock Strikes Twelve

Table of Contents

□

When The Clock Strikes Twelve

Dedicated to everyone
Who believed in me
when I did not have the
courage to
believe in myself.
Especially you.

□

When The Clock Strikes Twelve

When The Clock Strikes Twelve

Prologue

"Before I Became a Man"

I heard my conscious crying last night
Slumped like a bag of potatoes between a rock and a hard place
Whisky bottle tucked beneath his chin
With red blood shot eyes
I
Asked him if I could have a sit
He took a sip of his whisky before he asked me what I was doing in a place like this
And I told him
I told him that I was trying to find God in dark alleyways at gun point
With a King James Version of the Bible in my back pocket
The Star of David hanging from my neck
While spitting scriptures from the Quran
Trying to find a God
A God
That will forgive me
Because tonight I will sin

When The Clock Strikes Twelve

☐

BOOK ONE

When The Clock Strikes Twelve

When The Clock Strikes Twelve

"The Perks of Being a Wallflower"

You were confidence if it ever needed a spokesperson to leap from
You were flamingo if it ever needed a figure to look up to
You were women
Before boy knew that he was still boy
You were queen
Beehive drip honey from those lips
You were blossoming rose bush, with no thrones and smell of dandelion
You were cotton candy
You were
You were different
You were fresh air in a the room of familiarity
You were cinnamon toast crunch with cartoons on a Saturday morning
You were sunshine and sunset with both toes buried deep within the sand
You were peace
You were brave
You were oh so brave
You were heartbroken violinist
You were melody
You were Otis Redding on a Sunday morning
You were Otis Redding on a Sunday evening
You were Grandpop singing Otis Redding on his way to the job he had worked since he was 17
You were
You were dream
You were North Star
You were no fault in your stars
You were Augustus Waters
You were hope
You were game changing

When The Clock Strikes Twelve

You were James Bond Swagger Cool. Everything was
'trash" to you
You were let's go
You were "lesssssssss gooooo"
You were conversation from midnight to sun crept
over horizon
You were Perks of Being a Wallflower in background
You were innocence of two souls sleeping in the same
bed with comfort in the background
You were honest
You were open
You were you
And I was fool. I was irresponsible. I was messy
I was boy who did not know that he was still boy. Now
I am man who gives sorry ass apologizes
But apology none the less
I am growth
I am trying to do fucking better
I proclaim to be fucking better
I am who I am
You are who you were and forever will be
Beehive which dripeth honey from thy soul

When The Clock Strikes Twelve

"7 days"

When you speak to me of your dreams and aspirations
I watch as the Monday morning comes out of you
Reasons why alarm clock will not be your enemy but your bestfriend
Just listening to you, making my thoughts bubble like witches brew
As you conjure up the faith in me
Your eyes are so much Tuesday
Because they are not first nor are they last or even middle
But they hold taught in place like dam to tears and you keep moving forward
Even when the end is nowhere in sight
I imagine, your lips tasting like red wine on a Wednesday night
After a long, long, long day at work
Rejoicing in the break from reality yet knowing that there is still work to be done
I am convinced
That waking up next to you has to feel like a Thursday
Peace is over the horizon and all I have to do is keep on pushing and believing
Because I am so close
To happiness
Your touch, against the hallowed out tree stump of this body makes me feel full again
Like walking out on a Friday and simply being in love with the concept of time
Infatuated with the ways that you can use it to feed you
Your thighs hold every inch of Saturday between them
A night full of sin and sensation
Stimulations and vibrations
And one hell of a climax

When The Clock Strikes Twelve

The kind that will make you look at me the way that I
look at you when you are simply breathing
However, Sunday is and forever will be your smile
Because it reminds me that everything will be ok
That the sun will come up again showing off her
beauty
The moon will rise up again looking for his love
And the stars will watch their love story in amazement
And then when the shooting star screams across the
canvas of God
I will make a wish
It will be that there is always fire to the wood of your
imagination
As I stay up all night
Anticipating
Monday

When The Clock Strikes Twelve

"Dying Flowers in Water"

1. Love could not keep the depression away
It couldn't break down the root of it and will not keep the darkness out when the sun is highest in the sky.
2. Love could not keep the heat on during winters where the hardwood floor bites the whole of you. And hot plates become your savior. Wasn't enough to keep your mother from crying on your shoulder because you are 16 and still the closest thing to a man she has ever known.
3. Love will not keep you from second guessing your decisions of leaving college and disappointing a family who saw you as "The One", only to defend a country that only sees you as one. Nigga.
4. Love has never been enough to keep me and a women together long enough for the tea to brew fully and finally enjoy the beauty in each other's company long enough to laugh. It usually burns my tongue first.
5. Love did not stop me from letting you leave.
6. Love helped me find some light in the darkness. Just enough to make it to another day,
7. Love helped me find happiness in all of us sleeping in one room and holding my mother on my back as if her tears carved the Grand Canyon out of my soul. Such a beautiful site to see
8. Love gives me the memories of late night conversations on campus and a check to provide for my loved ones every two weeks. And opportunities to take back from those who have always taken from me. Nigga
9. Love still gives me hope that one day ill drink cold tea instead.
10. Love did not stop me from letting you leave.

When The Clock Strikes Twelve

"The First Man to Write About Love"

The first man to write about love had to have been a cynical man
With a plan so rooted in evil knowing that it would change the world forever
It would destroy empires and engulf itself into the mindset of even the greatest kings
It would be so enticing that even the strongest warriors would yearn for it
The first man to write about love must have been a master of sorcery
Conjuring up in his pot of clever words and bold metaphors, an ideology so struck with the taste of happiness on its tongue, that when you get close enough to feel it you mistake it as fulfillment
The first man to write about love must have been mesmerized by music
Making the sound of it acquire the empty spaces of your soul and play out like a theoretical symphony
Every note played representing another person believing that love is a beautiful, mind blowing and heart accelerating thing
The first man to write about love must have watched God create Adam and Eve and saw Adam's eyes the first time he glanced at his rib that used to be
The first man to write about love had to have been an alcoholic
His mind impaired and hands got sloppy with nothing to do
The first man to write about love had to have been heartbroken
In a way so divine that only TMH could heal himself
The first man to write about love
Must have been trying to get over you

When The Clock Strikes Twelve

"Rest Brown Boy Rest"

The car slows down to a complete stop
He glances over to his left at the memorial
Fresh flowers that were picked from the finest florist in town and teddy bears that looked like if they were placed in the right kids arms they could cure cancer
And dried blood in the middle of the street
There are no people marching in the middle of the street nor are there flames in the distance
It is quiet, yet the city is still enraged
He makes a face as if holding back a river of helplessness aft of his eyes
In that moment I watch as my brother died in front of me
Physically intact yet his spirit went asphalt black like the last time you remember playing freeze tag
There were no more childish ideas of hope inside of him
We sat there alongside the spot where his best friend was murdered
Where 6 bullets penetrated flesh and made a martyr of him
Nowadays I don't know if my brother still remembers how to pray
So on nights when I build up the courage to I pray for him
I'm hoping he can find the will to do so too
Because since that day he has had a bend in his spine
And he doesn't smile as often, forgetting that his voice could turn water to wine
You see
I met Mike once
Dapped up his hand and spoke kind words to his grandmother
My brother was family there

When The Clock Strikes Twelve

As close to home as I have ever seen him
So as we sat in the car with my brother's heart at his
feet I couldn't find the words to comfort him
I come to the conclusion that there aren't any
He tells me that Mike Mike said he felt like "he was
about to be famous for something soon,
He just didn't know for what"
None of us thought it would have been for this
None of us thought it would have been for this
Rest in peace Mike Brown

When The Clock Strikes Twelve

"To The Man That is Going to Replace Me"

Have you told her that you loved her today?
She needs to hear that
Reassurance that another human being believes in her
and can handle the weight of her insecurities on his
shoulders
Levitating the parts that are cracks in her soul keeping
her all together
She doesn't use lotion
Most times when she gets out the shower so be
careful because you might feel a sand paper texture if
you try to cuddle
Tease here about it
Or better yet rub it onto her back and moisturize her
entire body
Lord knows that she will need it
Hold her tight at night
You will turn into other positions but she will refuse so
you'll always end up behind her with your arms
wrapped, warmth will take over you.
She is the definition of a home body
She will only go out if you tell her you will take her
This is a blessing and a curse of its own
Because you won't have to worry about her safety
however, if you go out you won't enjoy your night
Do not buy her Netflix
She will Grey's Anatomy her life away
Stay on her head about school because she gets easily
distracted and often she is lazy
She is still a big baby when it comes to thunderstorms
Pray with her
Pray for her
Teach her the way with your heart, body and soul
Never slack off
Never get comfortable

When The Clock Strikes Twelve

Never think that you have everything under control
Never think that the devil hasn't whispered other names in her ear or won't bring other men to her bed
Love her with all of your heart
Or another man will

When The Clock Strikes Twelve

"Gypsy Eyes"

I held her tight like dawn holds mornings
Like babies hold fingers
Like tank-less divers hold air
Like the sky holds the clouds
Like the earth holds my feet
Like my feet hold me
Like saints hold the bible
Like sinners hold the bible
Like God holds prayers
Like Adams Ribs once held Eve
I saw life in her
Born again through breathe, her voice spoke rivers
through mountains and carved the Grand Canyon out
of me
I was only mere mortal
Forsaken from the fortress of my soul I became
destined for destruction
Determined to destroy myself by diluting my fears in
the tears of her being
What power did she have?
What hold did she have on me?
As strong as the possibility of strength itself
Or the possibility of falling in love with the possibility
of falling in love
We never made sense
Only cosmos on canvass created by cement
foundations
Creatures we were
But her eyes
Still wake up my butterflies
And they hold the wind
And dance in the pits of my stomach

When The Clock Strikes Twelve

"Warrior Eyes"

She held me like dusk holds night
Like hopeless holds romance
Like keys hold direction
Like universe holds existence
Like children hold naïve
Like heart holds beat
Like beat holds sound
Like saints hold the bible
Like sinners hold the bible
Like God holds prayer
Like Eve held Adam's eyes at first glance
She saw life in me
Spoke to me as if I could water the dying Eden of love
that once blossomed inside of her and turn it into the
Amazon
As if I could eliminate the experience of failure
As if my words could lunge love and lust through
worms holes and somehow lay upon her luscious lips
As if infinite internal insecurities that immortalize her
entity no longer mattered
We always made sense to her
My touch still warms her furnace
Awakening the dragon that lay dormant
I can hear him breathing life into me now
Exhale I will not
Ever

When The Clock Strikes Twelve

"When the Walls of Jericho Fell"

The echo from the telephone pierced the darkness
It was the bartender calling me again
My Guardian Angel had one too many drinks
And was reciting nonsense
Like love
Like I tried to save him
Like quit fantasizing about peace through death
Think about your sister's smile
Why doesn't he pray anymore?
Like why won't he listen?
Like why won't he see the signs?
I pulled up to the door and dragged him into the car
We both starred at each other
Looking at the only reason why the other was existing
in the first place
Before I could speak he asked me "do you find beauty
in pain?"
I told him "I find content in being comfortable with all
that I have ever known"
I have grown accustomed to the sound of hearts
shattering behind rib cages
Veins pumping oxygen to shivered up lungs
And eyes that no longer hold Atlantis between them
I asked him if "Do you find pleasure in watching my
sadness consume me?"
He replied "I am only trying to make you stronger"
Then I wondered how that could be true when my
reflection doesn't even fulfill me the same
I can't even step into my feelings like I used to
They have become too small to contain me
I'm numb
Forgetting what it's like to love,
To trust
To be

When The Clock Strikes Twelve

Human

When The Clock Strikes Twelve

"Communication"

She twirls her neck in rotation on que when she asks
"What's wrong" and I reply with nothing
Hands cocked in a ready position to express her
emotions in a sign language that only black
grandmothers have mastered
Here goes another argument
As man I have been trained to hide my emotions like
a bad credit score before a wedding day
Only being able to express angry to destroy and
conquer anything that comes in my path
Even you
So I apologize in advance that my quietness after a
long day feels like a stampede of fearful gazelle on the
plains of your heart
I'm terrified that if I express to you my sadness
Or if I express the self-doubt that I have inside of me
Or if I cry before your eyes
I'm afraid that you won't believe in superman
anymore
That I no longer will be your hero
Only human
And I don't know if that's enough
But I'm learning to allow you to be my kryptonite
Just believe in me
Work with me
And let the one above our heads handle the rest

When The Clock Strikes Twelve

"An Ode to Things I Will Never Understand"

The first time a man touched the apple between the Eden of her thighs
She wasn't tall enough to reach her favorite cereal
Wasn't old enough to vote
Hadn't driven her first car
Let alone had her first kiss
Until his lips pressed against hers feeling like fire to her skin. An inferno of things she was too young to understand
So it's no coincidence that her eyes still burn when she thinks about him
The man that would creep into her bedroom and touch her in places that no one else was supposed to see
Would tell her that if she told anyone they wouldn't believe her and that he would harm her mother
She loved her mother
And her parents always told her it's not ok to lie and she didn't want to disappoint them
So her lips became watertight doors on warships. No flood would come to harm her household
She would only drown silently in her secrets and in sweat beneath him
It started off as a simple touch and developed into something that hurts her to remember her silence was a sword in a dark room
No matter how hard she swung it at anything she would only be at war with herself
She became a refugee in her own skin
Trying to find a home because the person the world knew she wasn't who she was
She was only a crooked smile
Dying to talk to someone
Dying to tell someone what happened

When The Clock Strikes Twelve

When she was alone she would cuss at the sky asking
her guardian angel why he wouldn't protect her from
the monster he kept putting inside her
This isn't like the creatures in the books she reads at
school
This is much sinister
This is evil
This poem isn't a super hero poem
This isn't a poem with all the answers
This is an ears poem
Listen to the sounds of the cracks in their voices
Watch the shadows behind their smiles
They need you more than ever now
Become an expert in understanding the silence
In protecting our princess from the serpents after the
apple in their Garden of Eden
Do no judge them
Because it is not their fault
It is not your fault

When The Clock Strikes Twelve

"Untitled"

Sometimes you are so broken that when life throws you lemons you don't have the strength to make Lemonade
And that's ok too
One day you will

When The Clock Strikes Twelve

☐
"Lovehall Session 1"

Say baby, Can I be your slave?
Dig deep into your soul and find sanctuary in your rib
cage
This moment is captured in time
To mere man it is only sex
But to the Gods above we are in the midst of the Big
Bang
Your moans are becoming galaxies
Your eyes are holding life in them
And your orgasms resemble constellations
And the arch in your back is like a shooting star
Yet all I'm wishing on is that you continue to throw it
back on me

When The Clock Strikes Twelve

"No One Hears the Lion Crying"

I've been "handling" things since my thoughts could reminisce
My shoulders are mountain landscape hard from the weight of the world finding refuge on them
My spine indestructible from everyone around me leaning upon it
My feet are cement in the pavement
I shall not move
I've become accustomed, to being Alpha and Omega for those around me
The first one to give up his breath and the last one to breathe
I am unsure on what pain is
All I know...is that I can "handle" it
I stopped imagining things prematurely
I used to be able to create empires of happiness when I closed my eyes
Then one day
I grew up

When The Clock Strikes Twelve

"Those Eyes"

1. I've never looked into a pair of eyes that could hold home my soul the way that yours do. Captivated in them to the point that most times when we make eye contact I forget how to do basic human functions. Like breath...Or blink....Or move.

2. When I look at you I see everything that is wrong with me and everything that is right with me in the same instance. An overwhelming feeling that causes the Nile of my eyes to leak out onto the plateau of my face.

3. You bring out every emotion I have wrapped in the mummy of my heart. Yet you don't take any treasure from the tomb, you only examine the walls of my chest, deciphering the hieroglyphics, to understand the ones before you and how you can learn from their mistakes and love me in a way that I've never been loved before.

4. You are so damn beautiful. You are the prettiest girl in the world and I become overwhelmed with nervousness that other people see it to. And I cry most times because I don't want to lose you.

5. I can't imagine waking up without those eyes looking at me. And saying "I will always love you".

When The Clock Strikes Twelve

"Conversations with God"

God was a beaten man
His skin was as bright as midnight
His hands were as rough as the first break up
And I could hear in his voice the sound of forgotten
aspirations and almost accomplished dreams
He approached me
Shuttle
Yet with the command of roman generals
Excuse me young man
Can ... Can...I talk to you for a minute?
I saw in his face desperation and I knew what was
going to happen next yet
I said yeah
He sat down next to me and spoke from a place most
people will never be blessed nor cursed to ever speak
from
Ending with can you spare any change so I can eat
anything I'm, I'm starving
So I Reached into my pocket went passed the 20
dollar bill and handed all the 1's and spare change I
had
This equaled out to 6 bucks
Listen some more before I ended it with a God Bless,
a handshake, and a fight the power fist pump

When The Clock Strikes Twelve

"Wise Words"

My Grandfather taught me that a man has three obligations to his women:

He must PROVIDE for her
PROFESS his love for her
And PROTECT her from harm's way

When The Clock Strikes Twelve

"Indefinite"

The Law of Conservation of Energy states:
That Energy can neither be created nor destroyed;
rather, it transforms from one form to another
From a butterflies fluttering wings in Oklahoma to a
tsunami in Japan
It is indefinite
It will not cease to exist
It will only manifest into a biography of beauty
A story worth dying over
With an end that only begins again
You see it will decay and feed the soil to give birth to
an array of sunflowers in spring
The Law of Conservation of Energy is just a scientists
fancy, Harvard taught, cups of tea and philosophy,
metaphor
For Love
For Example
It is impossible to fall in love with someone
1 Being that gravity allows for limitations
So to fall means that there will be an end and we
know that energy or (love) is endless and limitless on
what it can become
And 2
You already loved them before you meet them
You are not god and cannot create such a force
A ripple in time whenever you see each other
Every night that you prayed for someone to love you
God was already molding them
Preparing them
Softening there heart to allow for your soul to rest on
You see Love transforms
From your first real kiss at 13

When The Clock Strikes Twelve

Outside of a church minutes after the sun rested its eyes
Under a maple tree with branches big enough to hide your innocence from the world
With a girl who you just knew was "the one"
The first time you will kiss the cheeks of a human that you helped create
And thank God for giving life into
And it reminds you of when you were 8 and you and your farther rode through the city bobbing your heads to Nellyville
Rejoicing in serenity
It is a cycle
Of morality conquering evil
And allowing room for energy to fill the space and transform
From a glance across the room
To a "I love you too"
You see The Law of Conservation of love states:
That Love can neither be created nor destroyed; rather, it transforms from one form to another
From a tsunami in Japan to butterflies fluttering wings in Oklahoma
Love is indefinite

When The Clock Strikes Twelve

"Lust"

She was midnight sin across the canvas of my
bedroom
She arrived with the smell of everything tasteful in a
woman
Yet covered herself in the scent of guilt
She took her clothes off at the door
I watched as she simulated taking off her insecurities
Fully in trusted in me
I did not flinch one bit knowing that I would undress
yet leave mines on, soaked in pride this is just the
tenth one night stand with the same woman
Emotions would be detached from every tongue flick
Every neck kiss
This is only business
An exchange of temporary pleasure and fighting the
consequences of being too afraid of being alone
because depression feels the same way
Both all too familiar
Neither of us will speak on them however
Neither of us will mention the elephant in the room
Both of us will move like dying stars who don't want to
get to close however live the last bits of sun inside
that we have left
In hopes that maybe one day God will believe in
giving us another Big Bang and we can finally start
over
Until then
We will pray
Separately
Because praying together is too intimate and this isn't
Hollywood and we aren't in love and why would God
want to listen to us anyway?
Two lost souls

When The Clock Strikes Twelve

Who keep mistaking the Devils path as his own
One day things will all make sense
One day the moon will tell u it all. And u will thank it
One day the stars will finally talk back and you will thank them
One day your intentions and heart will connect. And everything will be everything
And you will thank them
Until then
I will use u as my paint brush covered in the midnight black of sin
And stroke
Across my canvas

When The Clock Strikes Twelve

"Prayers"

I am nowhere near a saint
There is no Gabrielle blowing a trumpet to let me in
God doesn't recognize me anymore
He doesn't know what I have become. I am filled with
so much anger
So much lust
So much confusion
I was born disobedient
I must have pissed off my guardian angel early on in
existing
He must have set a path before me and the human in
me cause me to stray
So in return he went back to heaven, snuck into Gods
office and placed all of my prayers on the block list
And God has been around since the beginning of time
so he's not that tech savvy. So he hasn't even noticed
Just convinced him that I must have run out of faith
Because lately I've been screaming for answers

When The Clock Strikes Twelve

"Liquid Courage"

My alter egos name is Twoun
He rarely makes an appearance
But when he does he liberates my mind in ways I normally couldn't imagine
You see Twoun does not just live life he makes his life worth living
He operates with no regrets
He breathes "Carpe diem"
And I envy him
After the third red cup filled with Hennessy and coke I can fill him oozing out of my mouth my words become less filtered and more honest and pure
I become less tense and more open and inviting
I no longer stress over my insecurities
I wear them like badges of honor daring anyone to challenge me
You see Twoun is my superhero
After the fifth cup he is in full effect
He becomes the life of the party
Worrying is for the worried and he's only worried about one thing and that's love.
Maybe it be expressed through fist pumps and blacks with his boys
Or hip holding and back bending movements with some women in the club
Or devouring what's in between her legs
He is unleashed
He is care free
He isn't concerned about "What if's"
He is only concerned about when and how
He is me
When I'm not over thinking every possibility
He is me
When I do not doubt all of my abilities

When The Clock Strikes Twelve

He is me
When everything doesn't have to make sense as long
as it makes change
And I need to learn how to be him
More

When The Clock Strikes Twelve

"To My Unborn Princess"

I keep picturing this little girl running towards me
She's bare foot
With two missing front teeth
She has her mother's eyes.
A Head full of pink and green barrettes and those little
balls that snap back like orange beauty supply combs
on early mornings before school
Arms reached out like her grandmothers, a safe haven
for me to lean into
I imagine
That she looks up to this man whose word is bond and
strut is just as concrete
Her father
A man of many actions and wisely chosen decisions
A man who's name along is the only contract needed
to hear before any deal
A man that I hope one day to be
For her
My 4 foot creation
Who likes to discuss the politics of her 8 pm bed time
over tea with snugglelifgus and Pete the frog
Standing her ground until I change my mind
And let her stay up with dad until she falls asleep at
7:30 pm in my arms
And I realize the beauty of it all....because I can
already see her being a lawyer
Or a doctor, Or a gymnast, musician, president , or
whatever she sets her mind to because she has her
grandfather's ambition, her uncles impulse, and her
aunties mindset in which she cannot take no for an
answer
She's brilliant

When The Clock Strikes Twelve

Smarter than I ever was at her age and I'm proud of her beyond belief
Her smile
Her smile can heal the pain of the work day that puts pressure on my back. And when she says daddy what's wrong? Cheer up, as she places her hands on my face
I know
I know that is God speaking through her
So to the women I will decide to spend the rest of my life with I thank you now for helping me create such a wonderful child
Our child
Because I....I keep envisioning my daughter in my dreams
She's bare foot
With two missing front teeth
She has her mother's eyes
A Head full of pink and green barrettes and those little balls that snap back like orange beauty supply combs on early mornings before school
Arms reached out like her grandmothers
A safe haven for me to lean into

When The Clock Strikes Twelve

"Octopus"

I have big feet
The kind that clowns envy
They flap around like otter tails
I am also clumsy
I have a tendency of breaking things that weren't
really broken but I tried to fix them so now they are
actually broken
I don't listen
I am impatient
And I'm slowly going bald
Slowly sadly bald
I am loving
I have a way with words like Davinci did with a brush
I am rock
I'm unbreakable
I am a leader
I am an octopus in the ocean.
Not because I have a thing for octopus's or anything
because that's weird
More so because an octopus can kill a shark and this
world is like the ocean
Filled with sharks, crabs, and strange creatures
However, I am the best there is
All traits that you would one day acquire
So when I was out in the middle of the ocean and I
got the message from your mother saying that you
were no longer in the pits of her stomach
That My Elohim had called you back before you took
your first breath
That this two bedroom apartment would echo not of a
child's laughter but of a want to be fathers tears
I didn't feel like much of an octopus anymore
I don't feel any more at all

When The Clock Strikes Twelve

A numbness that feels my veins and shreds apart my insides
I am disgusted with existing
I wish I never named you
Because now there is this little girl who is reaching up to me for me to hold her and every time I extend my arms she disappears and I'm back to reality that you are not here
I won't get to teach you how to take your first steps
Watching you stumble and fall because you are trying to maneuver your father's inheritance of big feet
I won't get to watch you spill spaghetti onto your shirt
I won't get to take you to your first day of school, watching you ignore my advice because you're a big kid now and you "got this"
I don't get to scream your name in the stands at your high school graduation, afterwards listening to you saying how you can't wait to do this and that, as I tell you not to grow up and be a kid as long as you can.
I won't get to give you advice as a father as we both sadly are bald....because... because I won't get to be one
My words are jumbled in my mind
I am Jell-O
I am broken
I have followed darkness into a terrifying place
I am no longer an octopus
More like a coral reef
Hard
And at a standby from a distant
Yet
I know
That I'm filled with so much life
I'm just scared to try to create it
Again
And I'm sorry

When The Clock Strikes Twelve

"LoveHall Session 2"

Tonight you will scream my name until God himself snatches the oxygen from within your lungs
I will eat the doubt out of you
You will no longer wonder if you are beautiful
You will always remember the tongue of the poet by the way I devour you
On days when your chest is heavy and you feel lost in this world you will sit back and make peace in this memory
Do not resist the temptation to moan
I will match the rhythm with ever back starch you plan to accomplish this evening
I aim to free those inner Demons u keep locked inside of your mind
Shut up and quit speaking
I will not let go
Your hair has become an extension to your soul and I plan to bathe in every inch of it
Each Michael Angelo stroke will caress your insecurities to the point that it doesn't matter if the lights are off or on
You still will cum
Now come
Absorb the tension in this room
Every breathe against your skin sends a tingle down your spine
Every bite against your skin sends a tingle down your spine
Every kiss against your skin sends a tingle down your spine
All good reasons because I plan on bending your back into the mattress so each tingle is like a warm up to the grand finale

When The Clock Strikes Twelve

Now fall into me.
Collapse onto my body
Find happiness in this moment
And know
This is only Session 2

When The Clock Strikes Twelve

When The Clock Strikes Twelve

When The Clock Strikes Twelve

"Chantella's Interlude"

Dear Stevens,

I have to get this off my chest before I go so uh here it goes... From the moment I met you I knew there was something different about you, who knew that you would be the one to turn my life upside down... Yes upside down. You make me feel like anything is possible. I've never met someone who can affect my emotions from more than 60 miles away better yet in the middle of the ocean. I could be in the middle of just giving up then I think about you and realize it was all worth it. The navy was worth it, ending my engagement was worth it, falling for you was worth it. I wish I didn't fuck up as much as I did, you really didn't deserve everything I put you through. But like you said this isn't a goodbye I'm just going to the store for a few years lmfao I just hope you're not starving when I get back. Don't forget to keep in touch.

-Chantella

When The Clock Strikes Twelve

BOOK TWO

When The Clock Strikes Twelve

☐

When The Clock Strikes Twelve

"My First Love"

We fell in love inside of a burning room
The floor was buckling, the roof was about to collapse
and the smoke was thickening
Yet ....I asked you to dance
With two left feet and no rhythm I attempted to waltz
with you
We stumbled and tripped over each other but none of
it mattered because we were enticed with the idea of
never being lonely again
It consumed our better judgement

When The Clock Strikes Twelve

"10 Reasons Why I Hate Poetry"

1. It reminds me every day, every hour, and every minute that my mind wonders off. That I will make beauty out of things that others would consider ugly. Like the homeless man with a beer, in the cold, under the freeway who his wiser than any college professor. Or the woman who stays at home with a house full of trash. You would call her a hoarder. I just see a woman who is trying to fill the empty corridors of her place of refuge in hope to keep the quiet out. It is a curse that keeps me from living in reality.

2. It makes me believe that maybe just maybe if the right metaphor slides across my tongue and I speak it out loud in a room full of strangers that it will change someone's life. It makes me think that "maybe I can save someone today". Even though my cape doesn't fit the same way that it used to.

3. I am a love poet who knows nothing about love. I am a man who doesn't know how to let someone love me.

4. I haven't watched "Love Jones" in almost a year now.

5. Poetry isn't a night light. I am still afraid of the dark. Not being able to see what is in front of me. Being lost in a mirage of lonely. Reaching out into a room full of question marks and desperation.

When The Clock Strikes Twelve

6. I can name the people on one hand who still read my poetry. The ganger that once was no longer exists. The rooms full of people to come and see me perform my god given talent are now empty. Which makes me question was it ever me in the first place? Or was it the excitement of new that soon wore off. Was my moment of glory like a wave beating against the shoreline? I thought I was one being refreshed by now I watch as it fleas back into the ocean.

7. It hasn't fixed anything. It hasn't paid a light bill. It hasn't helped me in knowing myself. It hasn't protected the ones that I love. It just always feels my pockets with hope and the more life I love the more I know it will not be enough.

8. Poetry was once a way to express myself. It was an excuse to get on stage and let someone know that they mean something to me. To let someone know that they hurt me. To let the world know that I suffer to. To win people's hearts. To calm ones soul. It was a brief moment. My words made me feel as if I took a cigarette break and shared the relationship I had with peace with the world.

9. I question if it still has any abilities. Or did real life kick in and I just stopped dreaming.
10. Poetry doesn't love me anymore.

When The Clock Strikes Twelve

"10 Reasons Why I Write Love Poems"

1. I know nothing about love. Over the years I have acquired different ideologies on the phenomenon but nothing really sticks. No matter how hard I try to comprehend it the concept devours all sense of reality I thought that I had. So poetry helps me compensate for the lack of.

2. My first heart break. This moment in my life is pivotal. The first time I realized some women have bites like Cobras. And their promises aren't sturdy enough to hold back your dam of tears. She left me for another man. In front of me. In front of her family. In front of our friends. Made refuge on his lap and looked at me as if she felt pity for me. A small helpless puppy. I've never looked at a woman the same sense.

3. I become overwhelmed with bravery. Expressing my feelings carefree without any reason to feel pressured or feel insignificant. The only thing that matters in that moment is "honest expression" and honestly I feel invincible. Like no mere being could destroy my gift. God is watching over me.

4. It helps me connect with God. On days when I feel like I no longer matter in the grand scheme of things. On days when my life feels useless. As if I have no purpose. I'll write on the concept of love and suddenly I can feel Gods presence.

When The Clock Strikes Twelve

5. She cried in my arms the day I dropped her off at her ship. Her home port was shifting and I knew that I may not ever see her again. I cried in the car on the ride home. Yet the whole time she was here I pretended that she meant nothing to me. That' she was only a booty call that I called every day and got mad at on days that she couldn't make it. A booty call that I would hold tight at night like fog holds the horizon. A booty call that is over me. I learned to be honest from that situation and to tell someone how you honestly feel about them. Regardless of the circumstances or opinions of others. Because once they are gone they are gone. And you will still be there. Waiting.

6. I told myself I would never hurt a woman the way that my father has hurt my mother. I would cherish them and treat them like queens of the universe. A value that I have applied my entire life. "How could he leave my mom and me, alone?" I would ask myself this frequently. I'm 22 now and I finally understand his reasoning. And I'm glad that he did. But now. Who am I? My life is changing. What I value and believe is changing. What I stand for is changing. Trying to be comfortable with being uncomfortable.

7. Sex. I get lost between the legs of a women's body. Grabbing and pulling on her hair. Kissing and sucking on places that only few will ever see. And staring into each other's eyes. I like that sweet romantic making love shit.

8. Because I drink. Whisky helps me open up my "third eye" in ways meditation never has. It brings out all of my deepest darkest secrets. It frees me from the restrictions of society. Nothing even matters.

When The Clock Strikes Twelve

9. I feel pain. Usually other people's pain. It helps me sort out the mess that I have created in my head. Over thinking about over thinking about over thinking poetry puts the triangles in the triangles and the squares in the squares.

10. It is as close to second chances as I will ever obtain. As close to honesty as my pride allows it. And my pride doesn't allow many things.

When The Clock Strikes Twelve

"Confessions from a Decent Man (Thoughts in poem form)"

Being called perfect used to feel like a blessing to me. I would pride myself in the honor. I would Strut through rooms as if to say "look at me, I am the perfect man". I am kind, smart, driven, funny, charming, and even a little cute if I say so myself. All things that are good in a man. Right? ... Right?

Wrong.

People fall in love with the image of me. I would stand on stage and bleed my soul into a microphone and women would place their fantasies on me. Forgetting the fact that sometimes I lie to. That sometimes I make you feel bad like your ex used to. That sometimes there is nothing poetic about me. It's just me. An imperfect man who can admit that my shit stinks to.

Yet no one seems to believe that I can be like a normal man and see it through.

Maybe that's why _____ told me she could never be with me because she didn't deserve a man like me.

_____ cheated on me and told me I treated her to good.

_____ made me wait two years to feel the warmth of the inside of her body because "she wanted to do this right" but turned around and got pregnant from a man she knew for 2 weeks.

When The Clock Strikes Twelve

Or maybe _____ had really low self-esteem and honestly felt like she didn't deserve to be treated well.

Plus in college _____ asked me to give her another chance because she was young and dumb and didn't realize what she had in front of her.

And maybe _____ really felt low in her life and I was the only thing that felt "right" so she had to cherish it. Probably why she called me last week after a year of not talking just to tell me she still wanted to spend the rest of her life with me.

If all of this is true I really suck in picking women. Or maybe my heart is way too big and I try to love the hurt out of others. Or maybe both.

I started dogging women in the 12th grade. I became an instant success story. Women would come out of the woodworks to get a glimpse of me. By college I had perfected the skill. It wasn't hard anymore. But somewhere between 19-21 I decided that it wasn't me. And decided to stop fucking everything. But only the right thing. A woman I would spend the rest of my life with. Things didn't work out the way I planned them.

At 21 I had all the answers. I didn't listen to any advice any one told me and I made mistakes. I'm still making mistakes. But I'm learning. And improving. And can honestly say I don't regret anything. Because without everything that has happened to me I wouldn't be me. And I'm glad to be me. Mr. (im)perfect

When The Clock Strikes Twelve

"Letter from Adam"

Dear Sons,

Do not become a captive of her eyes
You will become mesmerized because The Most High
put everything that was breath taking in them
Do not become lost in the sound of her voice and the
taste of her lips.
I know they both can be oh so magnificent
Son
She is one with you
She is not an addition to you however she was made
from a rib inside of you
Therefore you both are one
Love the Sin out of her
And she will make you a man of God

When The Clock Strikes Twelve

"In the Beginning"

For every breathless moment that slithers down your
chest and collapses in your lungs
Think of me
Taking your breath away
Again
As if it was the first time
And just know
That in that moment
You are genesis
You are the beginning
Of everything that will make me happy ever after
I will reach into the darkness and call upon you in my
dreams
I will NEED you
I am an addict
To your love

When The Clock Strikes Twelve

"Scream"

Your legs shatter beneath you
Glass like
Trembling from the mining of your abdominal
Your lungs operate in overdrive
Speeding through the moment trying to catch your breath
Sweat dripping down the outline of your spine
Hands gripping the closest thing in sight
You beg of me not to stop
And I continue to elevate your soul
And then I turn you around and position you in a queen's stance
And bury my face between your thighs
And get lost in the grave of you
And get lost in the embrace from you
And get lost in the taste of you
Your eyes
Light up like the Fourth of July
Between the seconds that they are not curling behind your eyelids
I am determined to make you remember me
To know what it feels like to have a man cherish you spiritually, mentally, and physically.
To know what it is like to have someone focus on your pleasure
To have a man strong enough to submit his own selfish needs for you
All so that you can climax
And cum
Again

When The Clock Strikes Twelve

"Confessions from a Decent Man Part 2 (Thoughts in poem form)"

_____ found god

_____ found god

_____ found god

_____ is happy

_____ is happy

_____ doesn't date black men anymore

And _____ has forgotten that I even exist

I am only a pit spot

A brief moment in time where women find everything they have ever wanted in a man but not

I push them to their true identity

I break them apart into a million pieces

And repeatedly mend them back together again

I left _____ for her "best friend" In which pushed her to lose her virginity to a man who didn't deserve her temple which led to a slippery slope until she fell into gods arms and oh how he has held her ever so tight sense .

When The Clock Strikes Twelve

I opened the gates of _____ only to disappear into the distance. I met her mother. I supported her. Told her she was beautiful. Snuck between her legs and then faded into black.

She found god that summer and has never looked back.

I hate myself every day for what I did to _____. I dangled her around for years lying and hiding the truth. She deserved better than me. I broke her. To a point I don't know if she'll ever fully recover. But now god shields her from all of my fuckery. And she is happy.

I tried to take _____ virginity at a fucking restroom. She should hate my soul. But instead she still speaks kind words as she sits on her boyfriend's lap

I connected with _____ on a spiritual level. We vibed like in sync melodies. I broke her heart to. Lied about the idea of marriage

I'm glad she's happy now to

I treated _____ as if her virginity was a bargaining tool. That if she didn't give it to me on the set date then there was no need for us to dance under the stars that night. She never forgave

And I treated _____ as if she was only a piece of meat but every night she didn't come over to my room a piece of me would die inside

So most mornings I wake up and gaze into darkness

When The Clock Strikes Twelve

And I can still hear the wind snapping from their tears

And I hate myself for it

When The Clock Strikes Twelve

"Black Women is God"

Two things are definite in this world
The first
Being the sun will rise at dawn, rest its light upon the skyline, and will awaken the world with a vigorous roar
The second
Being that I will be famished
My tongue will be yearning to taste you again
It's only fulfillment will be in consuming you
I will lay my fingers in between the crevices of your thighs
I will drown every corner of your vulva with passionate licks
Every inch of you will inhale my spirit underneath your breath
No mere moan will suffice
I want to hear my name claw its way out of your chest, starch against the back of your throat, and when you finally shout it out it's more of a jumbled array of sounds more than it is a calling
But I know "Fuck" screamed into those four walls is your way of saying "I love you"
Do you remember the first time my lips engulfed you?
The first time I cradled you in my mouth?
The first time my saliva bathed you?
I want you to play back every encounter we have ever had and hold tight that second before you exploded onto the mattress
And close your eyes and count to 10
1. Now remember the way your body vibrated beneath me. Earthquake like motion with every kiss
2. Touch your skin and remember the way mines felt pressed on top of you.

When The Clock Strikes Twelve

3. Imagine my lips showing attention to your inner being

4. The way that I would hold one breast in my hand and the other would be restraining you down. Showing you that I am in charge yet admiring the beauty that is women

5. Are you ready to release?

6. The way my tongue strokes against the canvas of your body. I painted the Mona Lisa when I devoured you

7. The way it feels when I slide my fingers inside of you searching for gold

8. I make love to you in a way that only poets could write about. Bodies like waves beating onto the shore line

9. Breath

10. We rest. You lay with thoughts of forever on your mind. As I ponder about all of the opportunities. Waiting. For the sun to awaken the monster in me

When The Clock Strikes Twelve

"Howling at the Moon"

Sometimes I stare at you
You of course respond with an inquisitive "what"?
I immediately tell you that the only reason I got lost in
your eyes was because I was in deep thought
Or mere admiration to defuse the awkwardness of the
situation
And sometimes...I really am
But to be honest
Most times I'm trying to permanently stitch that
moment into the blanket of memories in my mind
Trying to remember every beauty mark that finds
refuge upon your skin
Trying to remember the way that your smile curls
when you laugh
Trying to remember the way that the kinkiness of your
hair is a reflection of how you truly are behind closed
doors
 Just in case there comes a day when that moment
will no longer exist
In case god decides that we no longer will have space
and time to occupy each other's space and time
I can close my eyes and remember
What it was like
To be next to you
When I insist on our hands being held together
It isn't me just trying to be cute. Or romantic
I'm trying to tell you that I will protect you
Hold you taught like line
Shield away the troubles of the world
And yet still find time to become one with you
When I kiss your forehead
I'm trying to tell you that I cherish you
That to me, you are like roses on judgement day

When The Clock Strikes Twelve

Everything else around me is burning down and my life is in shambles
Yet I will take time in awe. And glance at you.
Because you are that beautiful
And I will know that everything will be ok
When I kiss your lips
Both of them
It is my way of being man enough to submit to you
To elevate you with my tongue
And calm you with my mouth
It is always an honor
When I am inside of you
I am home
Lost in the aura that's is you
I am content
Nothing else matters but that moment
And I know
That when you are away. I can always look into the night sky
That when I am away you can always look at the night sky
Because we share the moon
We pray
Hands together towards the heavens
Our prayers sound like Howls from wolves
Thanking God for this blessing of me and you

When The Clock Strikes Twelve

"Problem Child"

He sits
With hope in his eyes, a cigarette in his hand and pain
in his heart
He watches
As the suns face begins to retreat below the horizon
As waves crash onto the shoreline
They hold beach like single mother holds son
Like grandmother holds hymns
Like wind holds the echo of your tears
His body is foreign to rest
He doesn't sleep much anymore
Too busy pondering ideas
Collecting what ifs and stumbling over regrets
He flicks the ash from his cigarette
Says a prayer and hopes that god can still recognize
the sound of his voice
His soul reeks of sin
He is cursed of being man
Imperfect being he is
Impatiently waiting to be bestowed patience because
he doesn't believe the future will be better than this
He is convinced that he is meant to hold the burden of
love on his shoulders and heal the ones around him
Somewhere along the line he lost himself
Loving everyone else
He can't recognize his face anymore
Mirrors hurt
A Skelton of who he once was stares back at him with
so many questions
If only his reflection knew what his subconscious was
conjuring up
He probably would retreat into the horizon too
He takes the last puff of his cigarette and disappears
into the night

When The Clock Strikes Twelve

An abyss of sorrow inside of him
He is Indulging in emptiness
Becoming one
With darkness

When The Clock Strikes Twelve

"Giving up"

I am a battered man
Spine strong with insecurities and self-doubt
Hands tremble and feet slow to move
Heart sometimes too concrete to be in sync with the
beat of love
My mouth never releasing my tongue from the back of
my throat when I am hurting
Quite often..I am hurting
Emotions collected inside of a bottle in my mind
reading "pride... this is all you have left"
What all do I have left?

When The Clock Strikes Twelve

"Honesty"

Music is blasting in the background yet the room is consumed with the sound of silence
It is screaming at the top of its lungs
Scorching through the back of its throat is a fiery of words begging to be heard
Walls sweating from the tension in their body language
Floor thumping like heart beats
Air thick with unanswered thoughts
Both Anxious on the inside
The anticipation is overwhelming
But they lock eyes
And in that moment
They knew
Things would never be the same

When The Clock Strikes Twelve

"Dear Mom (Letter 1)"

There are more nights than fingers I have to count when you cried on my shoulder
I have always been a rock for you
And I feel selfish for wanting you to be a rock for me too
My junior year of high school I went from your son into a man
I remember coming home and seeing the eviction notice on the front door
I remember the man taking our money for the apartment he promised us and speeding off with it
It was all we had left to keep a roof over our head
We didn't catch him
I remember us being homeless
I ended up staying with my dad and everybody else stayed in a friend of yours attic
I felt weak for leaving you all alone without me.
And then I became ashamed of you for allowing that to happen to us
For allowing the man you were with at the time to stay there too
For not making him get a job and help out
For being weak
On the night of my first spoken word competition you did not stay the whole night
I made it to the second round
You said it was because you felt like I didn't want you there but I did
I always do
I need you there
I am your son
My senior year of high school I sleep for a year in your living room between an air mattress and a couch

When The Clock Strikes Twelve

There were days when the depression was to strong
and I wanted to die and I could not talk to you
On the night of my high school graduation you didn't
want to go to dinner and celebrate because my dad's
girlfriend was going to be there
I thought that was childish and immature but I did not
tell you that
I just wanted my entire family there
I wanted you there
You didn't help me with my FASFA
I got no money for college
I always tell myself if you had it you would have sent
it
But you didn't.
And my friend's parents didn't have it either but they
always sent them something
Or helped to pay for something
But I understand why you didn't
Because it's me
And you know I would figure it out
Everybody knows I will figure it out
I always do
I paid for everything on my own
And still sometimes sent money home
Nobody supported me going into the navy
Not even you
Yet everyone always wants the fruits of my labor
Including you
Most days mom I just want affection from you
I know you are tough
I know you are not the overly emotional type
And I'm sorry for wishing you were more motherly like
I know you try
I know that you do
I know that you are who you are and stuck in your
ways

When The Clock Strikes Twelve

I know you mean well
And I know that you would die for me in a heartbeat
I know that you are proud of me
I know that you had me young and were trying to figure out life alongside with me
I know that you are still learning now
And I'm working on forgiving you and not holding everything against you
I am working on understanding where you come from
I am working on loving you for you
And I am sorry if I ever make you feel like I don't love you
Because I do
I am just learning how to grow and accept all things of my life that made me
Even the ugly

When The Clock Strikes Twelve

"Lonely"

Two empty vessels
Gravitating around each other
Finding time to get lost in the spaces of nothingness
The crevices of shadows
Their Silence always speaks louder than their words
It fills the room with a melancholy conversation
Not sad
Not happy
But accepting that they are existing
And maneuvering through space and time
Trying not to fall in love
When all that they have is space and time
To develop
To become the result of a bizarre metamorphosis and
transform into
A metaphorical butterfly
Beautiful thing we have become
And I never will forget it
I will save every memory in my mind behind a vault
made of the hardest stone
So that on nights when the wolves are howling at the
moon
I will be replaying mornings I laughed with you
Afternoons I held you
And evening we cried together
And in that moment
I won't be lonely

When The Clock Strikes Twelve

"Get You (After Daniel Caesar)"

"And I'll take some time

Just to be thankful for

That I had days full of you

Your

Before it whines down into the memories

It's all just memories" Kali Uchis

Full.
Of moments when I hear god whispering in the patterns of your heart beat
As his son
Hearing your voice was confirmation of the Holy Spirit
Trinity in every moment we speak
Two souls slow dancing to the sound of possibilities
In a ball room with question mark floors
And chandeliers with crystal answers too high for either one of us to see
Who would want to see anyways?
We are too busy absorbing the moment
Your dress is sewed together with love and insecurities
And my suit is tailored to match the baggage I come with
The music is the sound of laughter and joy
The waiters are standing by with wine filled to the brim
And the cheese and crackers taste like "what ifs" and "buts"
But...we are still dancing
Flawlessly
Across the room
Not worried about anything else but that moment

When The Clock Strikes Twelve

Focused on the steps and not the outcome
Not caring if we look goofy or if people talk about the way that we move
The only thing that matters is that we move
Each step as gentle as the last or as concrete as the first
No princess and knight in shining armor
More like a man with a vision and a women with a plan that gravitate towards each other like moon to earth
All under the sun
The only difference is that the sun has fallen beneath the skyline but you are smiling and I can still fill sunshine
And the Butterflies in my stomach have transformed into cameras to capture this moment.
So that my heart will never forget
This memory
Forever thankful for the time that whines down into days
Full....Of you

When The Clock Strikes Twelve

"LoveHall Session 3"

You taste like everything that is good about a woman
I pick you up off of your feet and allow your thighs to
rest upon my shoulders as you reach for the ceiling
Devouring everything he made you second guess
about yourself
This is the grand finale
Tonight I will break you
I will bend you into positions that will make you feel
again
The numbness inside of you will be pounded into
nothingness
This is the moment the walls fall and the storm breaks
And I feel the moisture between your thighs
And you will be content with it
Eyes rolled back yet I still see the milky in them
I will watch as you find your peace
Your serenity
Your closure on things you have always wondered
about yourself
And confirm them with a simple kiss on the cheek
And say "yes, you really are that beautiful"
I will fuck a new level of confidence into you
No longer wondering "if" you can accomplish anything
you set your mind to, more like "when", because you
just came for the 4th time in a row and you still have
energy left
And if you can keep moving in this session you damn
sure can take over the world
Your screams will sound like Cries of victory
Yet I still will feel like I'm the one who won
And when you collapse after every climax you will fall
into arms soft enough to hold you on your worst days
and strong enough to push you back up to try again

When The Clock Strikes Twelve

No strings attached so that this spirit can always be held in your hands
Even when you feel at most alone
And every bite on your neck will confirm that
You have finally caught the "Love Jones"

When The Clock Strikes Twelve

"LO QUE SERÁ SERÁ"

When I told you that I loved you
I knew that you did not feel the same and I had already been bathing in the embarrassment of chasing you
I knew that it would bring more humiliation
But I still told you
Because if one of us died tonight, could the other live in the silence of screams saying "What if?", " I should have" or "If I had one more conversation I would say..."
I could not
You told me that I was the only one who cared about you
The only one to make you feel good when our lips touched
Or feel good when our lips touched
You told me I didn't know how important I was to you
You cried onto my shoulder as I held you into the night
Only for your heart to be vacant again once the sun rose in the morning
What a trifling game we played
You would build walls faster than these hands could take down
You were not ready for what my heart was trying to give
But my heart couldn't fathom a life without you in it
And for that I apologize
I have a tendency to treat things that I care about like water treats trees
Help grow into roots from seeds
And branches and leaves
Until the world around them needs their existence to breathe

When The Clock Strikes Twelve

I am a captive to romance
I should easily be able to get over you and move on
with my life
However,
If you called me today and asked me to start over and
try again
To forget all of the dumb things we did to each other
To forgive and move on
You would have me at hello
I will forever be a prisoner to your lips

When The Clock Strikes Twelve

When The Clock Strikes Twelve

ABOUT THE AUTHOR

Antwoun Stevens is currently serving in the United States Navy as a Yeoman. Antwoun is originally from St. Louis, MO. He is a father of a beautiful baby boy named Immanuel. Antwoun started off his career as a poet first with the art of Hip Hop. He loved music and how artists put words together. This eventually led to him becoming interested in spoken word poetry. This is the first book from this up and coming superstar and it will not be his last!

Facebook: Antwoun Stevens
Twitter: Loweljacobs7
Instagram: Loweljacobs7

When The Clock Strikes Twelve

Lyric's For the Soul

When The Clock Strikes Twelve

When The Clock Strikes Twelve

I am trying to let love go
But my chest is still drunk
dialing your smile
It misses your face resting
upon it
My heart is indebted to you

-Missing Forever

When The Clock Strikes Twelve

Last time we were in the same vicinity we had a threesome
It was me, you, and Hennessy
The sinful trinity
Thou knowest nothing Holy about

-Revelations

When The Clock Strikes Twelve

Whenever you would scream my name
I know God could hear you
He keeps putting your face in my dreams
On the 8th day he created you
On the 9th day we kissed

-Genesis

When The Clock Strikes Twelve

My son was born almost a month ago
My father still hasn't called to congratulate me
That cuts deeper then I acknowledge
Somehow he is still my hero

-Stevens

When The Clock Strikes Twelve

Depression is not a disease
It is not a disorder
It is an Uncle that daps
everyone up in the room
But somehow still does not
make his way to the door
It always stays longer then
you want it to

-Its 11:11pm

When The Clock Strikes Twelve

Growing up poor is like hunger

You fill yourself with all of these things to feel full again

But the feeling always comes back

It never feels like it is enough

-Searching for Gold

When The Clock Strikes Twelve

The difference between forever, eternity, and infinity is simple
Forever is a really long time
Eternity is an infinite duration
And infinity is an unlimited extent of time, space, or quantity
I will love you in the universes of all three

-Letter to my Son

When The Clock Strikes Twelve

When The Clock Strikes Twelve

A short preview from Antwoun Stevens' next project "Dawn".

"Dawn"

Somewhere between midnight and death he lays
In a pile of his vomit
Face planted and barely breathing
Way too drunk to move yet this is the quietest his mind has been since he could remember

If Jack Daniels and depression has taught me anything it is this; there are two things that are definite in this world. The first, being that we all will fall in love. Let it be a person, place, or thing. It is an overwhelming experience that consumes your entire being; a feeling of something "belonging" to you. The second is that we all will die. In that moment on my bathroom floor I was coming to a realization of both. I laid there in my own vomit romancing the idea of death, while reminiscing over the feeling of butterflies flying in the pits of my stomach. Neither concept was new to me. Being a knight in shining armor has always been a dream of mine. I've always wanted to sweep a woman off of her feet and make her feel something that only movies are made of. And when it comes to death, the Grim Reaper and I have been acquainted since as long as I can remember. The first time I met him I believed his offer and thought that he had my best interest at heart. So when I was in the third grade I told my teacher I wanted to kill myself. That was the first time I understood the power of words. Since then the Grim Reaper and I have been playing tug-a-war with the idea of existing and the loudness of silence. You were

When The Clock Strikes Twelve

Made in the USA
Lexington, KY
22 November 2017